Erotic Hypnosis

A Beginner's Crash Course (including femdom, and female-led relationships scripts)

By
Alexandra Morris

About Alexandra Morris

Hey,

Are you interested in the FLR-lifestyle? Searching for a mistress or Domina?

You've come to the right place.

I'm a Femdom-enthusiast and inspiring author. My mission is to spread the word about Femdom far and wide.

Check my books and visit my site alexandramorris.com.

Best,

Mrs. Alex

Table of Contents

Introduction: What is Erotic Hypnosis?

Erotic Hypnosis is the induction of a state of consciousness during which a person becomes highly open to suggestions for the purposes of sexual satisfaction. Now you're probably asking yourself, *"What on Earth does any of that mean?"* so let us break it down into its elements. To gain the most from this book, it is critical you enter with a complete and comprehensive understanding of erotic hypnosis.

Most of us *think* we understand what hypnosis is, but the popular cultural perception is wildly different from the actual practice. Hypnosis is not about mind control or performance art. It's not about tricking people into embarrassing behaviors or uncovering lost memories. Hypnosis is simply a form of therapy that can be used recreationally or clinically. As a respected author, I feel it is important for you to have all the facts. Any claims made in this book will be based on reality. By giving you accurate and pertinent information, your expectations will be accurate as well.

If you begin this book hoping to achieve hands-free orgasms instantly or to gain complete control over your sexual partner(s), you will leave disappointed. There are two important facts you need to know before continuing this book. Only 10% of people are highly susceptible to hypnotic suggestions, according to an article released by the Stanford Medicine News Center[1]. The good news is that the study also contains brain scans, which prove hypnotic suggestion has observable effects on the brain.

In addition to that low percentage, it should be noted hypnosis performed in clinical settings is performed by doctors and psychotherapists with college degrees, not Aleister, who works at the mystical supply store downtown. I will absolutely sit here and tell you hypnosis has demonstrable clinical benefits, especially when it comes to managing chronic pain, weight loss, PTSD, and addiction. But I won't pretend for a single second this book gives you the tools and training to make your significant other quit smoking.

What this book does give you is a beginner's crash course for performing recreational hypnosis safely and effectively. Just because you didn't achieve the 250 coursework hours necessary to be a certified hypnotherapist doesn't mean you and your partner can't benefit from understanding the fundamental principles of hypnosis. Much like how you don't need a degree in kinesiology to learn to run or lift weights, you don't need to be a certified hypnotherapist to benefit from understanding the practice.

If practiced and performed properly, erotic hypnosis will open an entirely new world of sexual satisfaction for you. More and more people are coming to erotic hypnosis for a myriad of reasons. Some people see the intrinsic Dominant/submissive dynamic in hypnosis and want to apply it to their own sexual relationships. Others enjoy the thought of relinquishing control, while others need an elaborate organization of kinks and rituals to perform at all.

The Benefits of Erotic Hypnosis
The Benefits of erotic hypnosis are many; hence, the entire book you're holding. When all safety precautions are followed, there is no wrong way to enjoy erotic hypnosis. Some people find it incredibly difficult to

enjoy sex. Sex should be about love, passion, pleasure, exploration, and devotion, but some people find those things terrifying. It's so strange to think how long humans have been having sex (literally since humans existed) and how we got it all twisted it up to a point many of us find it difficult to enjoy.

Stop me if any of these things have ever happened to you. You work all day, get home and immediately have to cook, clean, run errands, shuttle the kids somewhere, negotiate some bill on the phone, go grocery shopping, meet a client or family member, and by the time you get to bed, sex is the last thing on your mind. It literally happens to all of us. Stress and exhaustion are a deadly cocktail when it comes to your libido. Stress can literally inhibit sexual arousal and sexual response to the point of erectile dysfunction. In fact, studies indicate stress and anxiety are the leading cause of sexual dysfunction[2]! That just goes to show how much of an effect our mentality and consciousness can have on the machinations of our bodies.

It might not even be daily stress that makes sex difficult for us to enjoy. If you have a history of trauma that can be sexual and/or emotional, if you grew up in a shame-based religious household, or if your culture shames the idea of a woman having a sexual appetite, it can be extremely difficult if not impossible to enjoy sex. Fortunately, there are solutions. When dealing with people who have suffered trauma, it is extremely important to take every precaution possible and consult with a licensed therapist about your intentions.

No one can guarantee any form of therapy will have the desired results. Any specialist, book, or treatment program that promises results is lying. Every one of us is unique, and our minds and bodies will respond to things differently. What I can guarantee is results are possible. Many people have found intense and repeatable sexual satisfaction from erotic hypnosis. There is a relief for people who suffer from psychological, sexual dysfunction. Hypnosis is simply one of many tools that can be used to treat it, and it is an effective, non-invasive tool at that.

As far as femdom erotic hypnosis goes, some men may find it difficult to submit to another person, especially a woman. This is simply the nature of almost every human culture on Earth but is also the reason why so many men find female domination so tantalizing. It is a power balance so unique in human culture it borders on taboo. Some men will find hypnotic suggestion opens them up to the possibility of female domination or beginning a female-led relationship.

And if you can't find sexual satisfaction from hypnosis, you can still use the techniques in this book for mindfulness, guided meditation, self-awareness, and relaxation. Hypnosis is extremely close to meditation and is arguably a form of guided meditation with a narrow set of rules and intentions. There are many benefits to erotic hypnosis, and ironically the most important thing for you to do above all else is to keep an open mind.

1. Stanford Medicine News Center, *Study identifies brain areas altered during hypnotic trances*, Williams, Sarah C.P. July 2016 http://med.stanford.edu/news/all-news/2016/07/study-identifies-brain-areas-altered-during-hypnotic-trances.html

2. Healthline, *Can Stress and Anxiety Cause Erectile Dysfunction?*, Rogers, Graham M.D. November 2016 https://www.healthline.com/health/erectile-dysfunction-anxiety-stress

Chapter One: Female Domination aka Femdom

Now that we have a strong understanding of what hypnosis is and what you can hope to achieve with it in a sexual capacity let us now look towards female domination for a comprehensive understanding of femdom erotic hypnosis.

Domination and submission are two complementary roles sexual partners can undertake for the purposes of power exchange during sex. The Dominant is the active force in a relationship, controlling their partner to various limits, which are understood and agreed upon beforehand. A submissive relinquishes a portion of their control to their Dominant for the purposes of sexual and emotional satisfaction. These roles can apply outside the bedroom as well, but for the purposes of femdom erotic hypnosis, we will only discuss them in a sexual capacity. Bear in mind anyone can be a Dominant, submissive, or a switch, which means they swap between the two roles day-to-day, week-to-week, or even moment-to-moment in the same session.

Why would someone want to be Dominant or submissive? There are many reasons why someone would choose either or both roles. For those who experience anxiety, allowing others to make decisions for them or who may feel powerless outside the bedroom, being a Dominant allows them to assume a role where they have greater control over their circumstances than would usually be allotted to them. Bear in mind a Dominant only has as much control as their submissive cedes to them, and all limits and desires should be discussed beforehand. Many women gravitate to the role of Dominant because their personal life and/or culture doesn't afford them the level of power and agency they desire.

While being a Dominant seems to have instant appeal to most people (who wouldn't want to have more power and control of their lives?), there is also a large subset of people who desire no control or agency whatsoever. Some people feel great anxiety when circumstances are beyond their control. Submissives, on the other hand, feel great anxiety when they have too much power in a situation. If you have trouble making important decisions, telling people what to do, or sticking up for yourself, then you may be a submissive. During sex, a submissive relinquishes power to their Dominant and relishes in the joy and freedom of losing control to another person. Free of decision anxiety and the onus of pleasing their partner, they can act as a sex doll, having their partner's will inflicted upon them, knowing the bliss of surrender.

There is absolutely nothing wrong with being a Dominant or submissive. Desiring to be a Dominant does not mean you are bossy, controlling, or want to be in a mentally abusive relationship. On the same token, being submissive does not mean you are lazy or unwilling to contribute to your relationship. When done with consent and planning, a D/s sexual relationship is a joyous partnership to participate in. Both partners (assuming you're monogamous, and to save on word count, I'm going to refer to monogamous relationships from now on though these rules can easily apply to polyamorous relationships) will discover how much happier they are when their roles and boundaries are understood before sex even takes place. Sometimes during sex, there is a power struggle determining who will drive the action, take control, or dictate what happens next. In a D/s relationship, once the roles are understood and defined, that never happens.

One of the most important things to understand about D/s relationships is the roles never have to break down along gender lines. Archaic thinking would dictate the man is obviously the Dominant, and his female partner is automatically the submissive. Not even addressing the fact this discounts gay and lesbian couples, this narrow thinking can cause undue stress and anxiety for men who want to submit and for women who want to dominate. Let me make it perfectly clear, there is nothing wrong with a woman submitting or dominating, and the same applies to men as well as non-binary people.

You assume the role that makes you feel the most comfortable. Experiment with your partner. Tell each other how your role makes you feel. For those of you in a relationship with a female Dominant, you are experiencing femdom firsthand.

There is nothing intrinsically unique about submitting to a femdom. Women are just as capable as men when it comes to dominate their partners. What is unique about femdom is the cultural connotations around women. Many men find the idea of submitting to a woman absolutely tantalizing. Almost every culture portrays women as a passive, submissive gender, so the idea of a woman taking control of you may feel acutely erotic and taboo. It is a sad side effect of history, but many men find the prospect incredible. There are also men who are simply submissive, attracted to women, and prefer to have their female partner take control inside or outside the bedroom. This is what is known as a female-led relationship or FLR. Some men prefer FLR's for humiliation or because it suits their personality, neither of which is wrong as long as their female partner also enjoys their role in the relationship.

Chapter Two: Short History of Erotic Hypnosis

Before you can begin practicing hypnotic suggestion, it is important you understand where hypnosis came from and its storied history throughout the ages. Hypnosis has literally been around for thousands of years, but only received any kind of scientific scrutiny starting in the 1700s. The first known clinical use of hypnosis comes from what historians refer to as sleep temples that existed in ancient Egypt and ancient India over 4,000 years ago. These temples were a combination of church and hospital where a person was brought to pray and participate in a guided meditation in order to cure their afflictions in what is known as temple sleep.

The first medical journal to discuss hypnosis was written by the Persian physician Avicenna, known as The Book of Healing, which was published in 1027 C.E. Many people would be surprised to find out the use of hypnotism in western cultures completely revolved around magnets. This is where things get really interesting. A traveling Jesuit priest by the name of

Father Maximillian Hell (who was not an anime villain but in fact, a traveling healer) used magnets to treat the ailments of his followers. This caught the attention of Franz Mesmer, who coined the term "animal magnetism" and who we derive the word 'mesmerized' from.

Franz Mesmer believed the same forces that dictated the tides also dictated our health, and those energies existed in our bodies. He believed by adjusting or balancing the amount of "animal magnetism" in our bodies, he could cure a variety of maladies. It is important to understand animal magnetism in his time did not mean what it means today. He was simply describing energy or fluid he couldn't observe or detect but still had a great influence on our wellbeing.

His therapy, which was called mesmerism™, involved the use of magnets to move and control the animal magnetism in a patient's body and improve their health. His unfounded theory later dictated he could simply use his bare hands in the place of magnets since he had so much animal magnetism he didn't require magnets to treat patients. This, as you can imagine, caused a lot of problems. In what is remarkably similar to a reiki session, Franz Mesmer would gently rub his hands over a patient. In some combination of hypnotic suggestion and the placebo effect, many of his patients claimed to have been treated successfully by Mesmer, though he was forced out of Vienna when he failed to heal a famous musician.

Things only became stranger from there. Franz moved to Paris, and as part of the aristocracy, thanks to his advantageous marriage, he would see as many as 400 rich and powerful clients in a single day. His mesmeric treatments were like something out of a Robert E. Howard short story. Patients would be tended to in his dimly lit salon flooded with burning incense. At the center of the room was a strange machine called a baquet filled with glass and scraps of iron. The baquet looked like a wooden bathtub flipped upside down with metal spider legs coming out of it. Patients would sit around the baquet and hold hands as Mesmer flitted around the room in a lavender wizard's robe and rubbed his magnetic wizard wand over his patients. Aren't you glad you read this book?

As you can imagine, this caused a few problems for our old friend Franz Mesmer. One of his clients at the time was a woman named Marie Antoinette. Yes, that Marie Antoinette, wife of King Louis XVI. Ole' Lou didn't really approve of this utter insanity and created multiple commissions charged with finding out if animal magnetism even existed, one of which included Benjamin Franklin. Franz was furious and refused to participate in their scientific trials. As you may have guessed, the scientific commissions could not find proof animal magnetism existed. Franz left the country and later died in obscurity.

Thankfully, a more scrupulous physician named James Braid saved hypnotism from dying in obscurity like alchemy or the zune. James Braid was a legitimate physician who did serious and credible research into the phenomenon we now know today as hypnosis and even coined the term "hypnosis." Braid first witnessed mesmerism™ during a traveling show, and the mesmerist there allowed him to observe the patients who were mesmerized. Disliking the charlatan connotations of mesmerism, Braid coined the term "neuro-hypnotism" before he realized hypnosis doesn't actually put you to sleep like previously believed. He wanted to call the phenomenon mono-ideism, but that doesn't have quite the same ring to it. Braid observed a changed in the mental countenance of patients who focused their eyesight on a single, bright point such as lamp, candle, or mirror, a technique still used by hypnotherapists today. Because of Braid's extensive research and willingness to discuss his findings, he singlehandedly rescued hypnosis from obscurity and is considered by many to be the father of hypnotism.

The earliest reference to erotic hypnosis I have been able to find comes from a 1963 book called Perverse Crimes in History, wherein Robert Masters suggests erotic hypnosis can be used to overcome sexual dysfunction resulting from trauma in addition to creating hands-free orgasms and vivid, erotic hallucinations. These claims should all be taken with a pinch of salt, but it would also be safe to say erotic hypnosis has lasted as long as clinical hypnosis itself, considering there were rumors Franz Mesmer used it for his own, personal sexual satisfaction on some of his female patients.

This is why knowing your history is so important. You must respect the process and understand how destructive it can be as well as the negative connotations surrounding hypnosis. If you purchased or borrowed this book, clearly, you have at least a passing interest in hypnosis, but should understand your partner might not feel the same way. That is why it is critical you come armed with pertinent information. Only relatively recently has hypnosis been seen as a legitimate treatment, and even less is known or understood about its erotic applications. With the writing of this book, I am hoping to shed more light on this greatly misunderstood phenomenon and create a positive sexual experience for you and your partner.

Chapter Three: How to Perform a Session

While no single book can give you all the information you need to be a professional hypnotherapist, that doesn't mean you can't pick up enough technique to reap noticeable benefit from personal erotic hypnosis sessions at home. Don't worry about your level of education or prior experience. For your purposes, a beginner's guide is enough to see results. As long as you aren't charging people for this service or purporting to treat illnesses, you'll be fine.

The most important thing you can do is read and re-read this chapter and practice constantly. Don't expect huge results in your first attempt. Erotic hypnosis is a delicate yet intensive procedure. You could do everything right, but your partner may be unable to focus or have other worries on their minds. If you are unsuccessful your first time, that doesn't mean you will never be successful. There are other sources of learning besides this book.

I think one of the most important things we pick up as functioning adults, and a sign of confidence and trustworthiness is to go out and do our own research. No one book has all the answers. You found an excellent, approachable book to start with, but there are more intensive guides to further your learning. I'm so confident in the information presented in this book. I want you to go out and compare what I have told you what others have said in the field of erotic hypnosis. Don't take anything I say at face value. With those caveats out of the way, let's breakdown the steps of a successful hypnosis session.

Negotiate Limits and Boundaries

Before every single erotic hypnosis session, no matter how familiar you are with your partner, always check in to confirm where you and your partner's boundaries are. This is applicable even when you aren't practicing hypnosis. No matter how vanilla you consider your sex life, it is paramount you check in frequently to make sure both of you are comfortable with plans and past experiences.

Imagine if your partner felt stress and anxiety at the thought of being hypnotized, but you never gave them the opportunity to speak up until afterward? That would be a miserable experience for them and could sour them to ever participating again. Especially when it comes to surrendering power or control (in this case in the form of hypnotic suggestion), it is critical you and your partner are on the same page. Never attempt to force a nervous or unwilling participant into erotic hypnosis. If they are uncomfortable, then it is inappropriate to try.

In addition to establishing ease and comfort, limits, and safe words should be implemented as well. Discuss with your partner beforehand what they will be willing and unwilling to do under the influence of hypnotic suggestion. Typically you will receive a shortlist of undesirable tasks, but your partner is allowed as many limits as they need. In my experience, I find it helpful to establish soft limits and hard limits. Soft limits are generally kinkier things that require a certain mood (such as a hypnotic trance) in order to enjoy and participate in. These limits can be broken with your partner's permission. Hard limits, on the other hand, cannot be broken under any circumstances, and it is considered a massive violation of trust to do so.

Also, keep in mind the hypnotist has the same limits and right of refusal as their partner. If a hypnotist is uncomfortable making their partner perform a certain action or giving a specific suggestion, they are absolutely allowed to refuse. Limits are about comfort. They are not resources to be negotiated in your favor. Respect your partner and their desires.

Even when limits are established, events can transpire, which require an immediate pause in erotic activity. If someone develops anxiety or pain during a session, they need a way to stop it immediately. Saying 'no' or 'stop' is not sufficient as many people enjoy saying those things in the throes of passion for heightening forbidden feelings. To be safe, you and your partner should establish a safe word. Ideally, one or two syllables, something easy to pronounce, and a word that would not occur naturally during sex. In addition to a safe word, those practicing hypnosis should also have what is called a safe gesture. People who have been under the influence of hypnosis sometimes describe an inability to form words or conjure the word they wish to speak. In this circumstance, a distinct gesture should be employed if they find their situation untenable. Snapping fingers, clapping, or pulling your ear lobe are all simple gestures that can be employed as safe gestures to pause the action.

Induce a Trance

Each piece of the hypnosis procedure is equally important. When people think of hypnosis, they think of putting people into a trance, but negotiating comfort, implanting suggesting, and providing aftercare are crucial components of the erotic hypnosis process. Don't focus all your attention on induction and neglect the other pieces of the process.

The key component of induction is relaxation. Your goal during this phase of erotic hypnosis is to make your partner more relaxed and comfortable than they have ever been before and to eliminate any possible worries or distractions. To start, focus on physical relaxation, which can help with mental relaxation when it comes later. Have them lay or sit in their most comfortable position possible. This can be sitting on the couch, reclining in an armchair, or lying in bed. The exact position is not important, and everyone is different. What is important is they are as comfortable as possible. The last thing you want is for your partner to be thinking about back, foot, or shoulder pain when you are trying to induce a trance.

Some hypnotists use incense or candles as part of the relaxation process, but bear in mind you'll be using a scent as a focal point if you choose to do so. Either way, start by having your partner take a deep breath in through their nose and out through their mouth. Have them repeat this process several times. Let them take several deep breaths and gently bring them to a normal level of breathing. As you talk them through this, steadily lower the volume of your voice. Slow your cadence. This is a subconscious cue for them to relax. As you talk slower and gentler, subconsciously, they will become even more relaxed and move to a trance state. What you are essentially doing is making them more relaxed than they have ever been before.

To help relax their mind, have them focus on their breathing. Repeat this simple mantra, becoming quieter, and soft-spoken as the chant goes on, "Breath in through your nose, out through your mouth. In through your nose, out through your mouth." Repeat this several times. Then have them focus on their breathing. Direct them to focus their attention on the sound of their breathing, how the healing air relaxes their muscles and lowers their heart rate. Then put intense focus on the sound of breathing and only the sound.

One of the common pitfalls of hypnosis is when a practitioner instructs their subject to clear their mind. It's important to hypnotic implant suggestions, but human beings are absolutely terrible at clearing their minds. Your brain wants to think every second of every day. You must give your partner something incredibly simple and present to think about. Their focus can literally be anything as long as it's simple and doesn't raise questions when they think about it. You can have them focus on a candle, a piece of jewelry, a handkerchief, but not something like a song or painting, which might amplify their imagination instead of taming it.

At this point, your partner should be partially or fully induced in a hypnotic trance. To go all the way, you must enact a process called deepening. Now that they are relaxed and focused have them become even more relaxed and focused.

A strong technique for ultimate relaxation is what is called a body scan. Start at their toes, and describe to them an intense sensation of comfort and relaxation. Move to the feet, the ankles, shins, knees, thighs, hips, groin, stomach, chest, arms, you get the picture. Go slow. Take as much time as possible. Hypnosis is not about a quick fix. The slower and quieter you go, the more effective your deepening will be. At this point, your partner should be in a state of ultimate relaxation.

To focus their attention even more intensely, have them focus on what is called sub modalities. Sub modalities are a subset of the five primary senses. If focusing on a candle, focus on how bright it is, how it flickers, how small or large it is, specifically the flame. You are evaporating all their errant thoughts, which make hypnosis difficult and instead of having them focus on one thing with the utmost intensity. You are opening their mind up to receiving suggestions.

Hypnotic Suggestion

After relaxing their body and focusing their mind, now you can begin the process of hypnotic suggestion. This is the portion of hypnosis where your creativity can run wild. Bearing in mind, this book is designed for femdom erotic hypnosis, there are several strategies for making the most of your suggestions.

One technique is amplifying arousal. Create a series of associations with your partner to immerse them in female domination and your female further led relationship. Below are three suggestions you can use for positive association, but feel free to create your own.

- *"When you think of being dominated by women, you will feel intense erotic excitement."*
- *"Being in a female-led relationship fills you with joy and contentment."*
- *"The idea of being controlled by a woman causes you great arousal."*

Your goal is to create positive associations with female domination and heighten the erotic response your partner has to it. If your partner responds to aspects of BDSM like impact play, bondage, or humiliation, you can also create positive associations with these practices as well.

Another technique of hypnotic suggestion is guided visualization. Instead of implanting suggestions, you are implanting fantasies into your partner. This leaves room for limitless creativity and imagination, and the next chapter is completely dedicated to effectively creating your own script to recite to your partner.

Another technique you may enjoy is the implementation of triggers. Triggers are objects or actions that will trigger an erotic response in your partner. They can be new triggers, or you can reinforce triggers your partner already enjoys. Here are some examples.

- *"When you see me wear my red lipstick, you will feel submissive towards me."*

- *"When I put on my black corset, you will obey my every command."*
- *"You will become aroused whenever you think about submitting to me."*

The final technique involves creating new kinks in your partner. Just because your partner doesn't currently find a certain thing, erotic doesn't mean they can't be made to. Erotic hypnosis is the perfect technique for opening up their sexual palette. Try a few of these suggestions next time your partner is in a trance.

- *"From now on, you will find powerful women intensely erotic."*
- *"You will now find sexual arousal whenever you please me."*
- *"The idea of submitting to me fills you with sexual energy."*

An important thing to keep in mind when inducing a trance or to give hypnotic suggestions is that hypnosis will not work every time it is performed, especially when you and your partner are new to it. Some people simply cannot be hypnotized because they are too willful or doubtful of the process. Others may experience too much stress and anxiety on a certain night. Your partner may be worrying about other things or experience physical pain during a session. It may take several attempts to experience noticeable results. What is important is that you practice and learn all you can learn about hypnosis.

Aftercare

After any kind of sexual activity, it is of critical importance to provide aftercare for your partner. To bring them out of their trance, guide them back to a state of normalcy, returning their mental and physical sensations back to where you started before the session. It can be helpful to count them down as they leave their trance and finish with a clap or snap of your fingers, signaling to their brain the session is over.

If hypnosis becomes too effective, you may have to wipe suggestions from their minds. If your partner becomes too aroused but certain objects or actions, you might have to dismiss those suggestions before your hypnosis session ends. For example, "My knee-high boots no longer make you feel submissive."

Once your partner is out of their trance, they may not experience anything at all, or they may experience intense emotions. It is of critical importance you provide them physical and emotional comfort as they come out of their hypnosis session. This is what is known in the BDSM community as aftercare. Power exchanges can serve well up all kinds of intense emotions in a person, and it is your sworn duty as their sexual partner to provide them comfort if they need it. Make sure you schedule enough time in your session for aftercare. This is not a process that can be simply glossed over.

Even if your partner did not need aftercare during a previous session, they might require it this time or after a future session. The offer should always be on the table. There is no shame in needing to be comforted and reassured. Aftercare is an excellent time to bond with your partner outside a sexual setting. Have blankets and videos ready. Sometimes you may need to take their mind off their current emotions, so their favorite TV show or streaming series may afford an excellent distraction. Some subs become hungry or exhausted after a particularly long session. There's no reason not to stock up on their favorite foods and feed them afterward.

Hypnotic sessions can feel like an intense journey for the participants, both physically and emotionally. It is important you have comforts such as bedding, food, TV, and even stuffed animals close at hand should your submissive need them. This is not some afterthought you can choose not to participate in. Not only do you have a responsibility to comfort your partner after distress you advertently or inadvertently caused, but aftercare is also an integral part of the sexual experience. If you fail to provide these comforts after such an arduous emotional journey, you run the risk of damaging your relationship. You may also lose the chance of ever performing hypnosis again if you fail to be reliable when your partner comes out of their trance. All four portions of the hypnosis process are equally important. While induction and suggestion require specific technique and practice to master, negotiation and aftercare are simple tasks you should easily be able to provide.

Chapter Four: How to Write Your Own Hypnosis Script

Writing your own hypnosis script is not as difficult as you may initially believe. Even if you've never written anything since high school, anyone can write an effective hypnosis script with a few rules and techniques. You absolutely don't have to worry about grammar, spelling, or punctuation as you and your partner will be the only ones who ever see it.

Before I lay some tips on you, I'd like to suggest that if you're the hypnotist in your partnership, don't have your partner write the script. If your subject writes the script, their brain will be anticipating what is going to be said next instead of focusing on the words currently being said. Much in the same way that highly effective relaxation tracks contain no lyrics and don't repeat sections of melody, your subject should be focused on the meaning and effect of the words instead of the words themselves. They can offer suggestions about what they would like to see in a script, but having them write or co-write the script can reduce the effectiveness.

A large portion of the script involves retreading the techniques from the previous chapter. Feel free to mix and match induction techniques from earlier. Body scans and countdowns are effective and proven ways to induce a trance. Don't feel like you're cheating or being lazy by using the same induction techniques over and over. If a technique has proven effectiveness in your relationship, stick with it. There's no reason to change things out of some misguided obligation to avoid lazy writing. While I cannot give advice or advocate selling hypnosis scripts, for the purposes of your sexual relationship, repeating induction techniques is suitable for recreational purposes.

Bear in mind some induction techniques might be more effective when combined with certain suggestions and less effective when combined with others. Practice and experimentation are key to the effective technique as well as effective scripts. Don't put any pressure on yourself to get this perfect immediately. If you've never written a hypnosis script before, how can you expect to be great at it your first time?

Once you are satisfied with your induction, now you must consider what suggestions you would like to get across. As stated in the previous chapter, you have multiple styles of suggestion you can focus on or mix and match. Simple suggestions may involve reinforcing ideas and kinks your partner already finds arousing. Other suggestions may involve creating new associations between objects and behavior with sexual arousal. Finally, you can create a guided experience for your partner. One of the most intense things about hypnosis is how powerful visualizations become during a trance. This isn't simply sight and sound but all kinds of sensations, both physical and emotional.

Writing a script beforehand is an excellent way to create a vivid fantasy for your partner instead of relying on spontaneous creativity at the moment. With a script, you won't stumble or slow down as you struggle to continue their fantasy in their minds. Plus, with a script, you can practice in private or even memorize your words as if they were lines in a play. Some people prefer to spontaneously guide a fantasy, while others swear by a script. Neither is incorrect, and different things work for different people.

When creating a guided fantasy, this is an excellent time to get input from your sub. Find out what their fantasies are and have them describe their fantasies with as much detail as possible. When hypnosis is at its most effective, it can feel like you're really there inside the fantasy and experience the same emotions and physical sensations as if you really had a sexual encounter.

The Language of a Script

If there was a surefire way to be an excellent writer, there wouldn't be so many crappy books in circulation. You have the benefit of only needing to please one reader, in this case, a listener. As stated before, practice and experimentation lead to better scripts. But as you write, you should focus on the language of your script. Some professionals disdain the use of overly floral or descriptive language, but in a hypnotic script, that is exactly what you need to aim for. As a general rule of thumb, you want to focus on the five senses to make the experience as vivid as possible. The more senses you engage, the more your sub will feel like they are really there.

In addition to the five senses, also engage the sub modalities. Don't just focus on what they're seeing, but how big something is, how dark a room is, how soft something is, and the sensation of time passing.

The utmost importance should be placed on the sexual and emotional feelings of an experience. These hypnotic suggestions are designed to elicit a sexual and emotional response in your sub, but remember, they are in a trance and open to broader suggestions. With effective hypnosis, you can implant feelings of arousal in your sub without describing anything erotic. If they desire to feel small, weak, or feminine, describe those feelings to them. Effective hypnosis is about combining the feelings with the thoughts that generate those feelings. You're pushing on them from separate sides in order to create an intense swirl of emotional and sexual experience like a crucible in their mind.

Finally, be sure to leave room in your script for aftercare. You need to bring them out of their trance with all the care you used to put them in. Focus on soothing and pleasant emotions. Make their feelings and suggestions mild to help them cope with what they're experiencing. Take your time. There is no rush when it comes to hypnosis.

In our final three chapters, you will be able to read and use scripts already prepared for you and your partner. Feel free to alter these scripts to suit your needs, but remember the importance of good technique. Suggestions are not effective before inducing a trance, and aftercare is critical for the wellbeing of your partner.

Chapter Five: Femdom Script

"Breath in through your nose and out through your mouth. Breathe in through your nose and out through your mouth. In through your nose, out through your mouth. In through your nose, out through your mouth. Breathe in...And out. Breathe in...And out. Breathe slowly. A gentle breath.

"You slowly feel yourself becoming relaxed. Your body is gently relaxed. Just a little bit. Your tense muscles are loosening. The tension in your legs and back are easing. Feel the healing blood flow move through your muscles, easing pain and tension. Feel relaxation wash over you like a warm tide. The warmth starts in your toes. Imagine each of your toes alive with gentle warmth, relaxing. The warmth spreads through your feet, releasing ache and tension. Relaxation moves through your legs, easing your muscles. Your knees heal and relax. Feel the tension ease in your hips and back. Warmth spreads and relaxes you. Feel the rush of warm energy to your cock/pussy. Feel your sexual energy spark and smolder as your body receives healing warmth. The warm, healing energy moves up

your back. Your back relaxes, your shoulders rest, and you are completely relaxed. The muscles in your neck relax. You are soft, warm, and feel amazing. Amazing warmth floods through your body. Your face and ears filled with warmth. Your entire body is filled with warmth, washing over you.

"Imagine lying down in the surf, and warm ocean waves wash over you. Warm water gently cascading over your naked body, easing your pain and tension. Warm ocean waves enveloping you. The waves come and wash the pain out. The waves come in and out. In...and out. In...and out.

"You can feel your body floating. Floating on warm water, you are completely at rest. Your body is more relaxed than it has ever been before. Every muscle and joint in your body is loose. Loose like warm water running over smooth rocks. You are at peace. You are comfortable. You know comfort. You gently float down a warm stream knowing complete peace and comfort.

"Imagine the stream. Clearwater whispers over smooth stone. Focus on the water. Focus only on the water. The water is clear. Focus on the murmur as it flows over smooth stones. The gentle warm water flows. Focus on the clear water flowing. It flows. Focus your mind. Focus on the flowing, clear water. Focus. Take a deep breath in through your nose and out through your mouth. Breathe for me. Focus on the clear water flowing. Your mind is a clear stream flowing freely. Focus on the clear water. Take a deep breath. In through your nose, out through your mouth. Focus on the clear stream.

"Focus your mind. Focus on the stream. Your mind is a clear running stream. Relax. Open yourself up. Open yourself to my suggestions. You are more relaxed than you have ever been before, and your mind is open to me. Your mind is open to me. Focus on the sound of my voice. Focus on my voice. Focus...on my voice. Listen to the sound of my voice. Listen. You will obey the sound of my voice. You will obey my words. My words will become your thoughts. Listen to my words. Listen. Listen. Listen.

"You are feeling submissive. In your heart and mind, you can feel submission blooming like a beautiful flower. Your deepest desire is to submit to me. You were born to submit, and you have chosen to submit to me. You are submissive, and that makes you beautiful. In your heart, you know you are a submissive. Feel the weight of my authority over you like a heavy blanket. The blanket is warm and comforts you. It weighs you down. Feel how heavy it is. You are warm and comforted under the weight of my authority. In your heart, you feel peace and comfort when you submit to me.

"You feel weaker. You feel the weight of my dominance, pushing you under me. You give yourself freely to me. Feel your weakness, your lack of strength. Feel yourself weakening. Relish in how delicate you feel. You are a beautiful submissive, weak, vulnerable, and free. Feel the weakness and submission move through your body. You will submit to me and only me. Your muscles are soft, and your body yields to me.

"When you hear the sound of my voice, you will feel submissive. When you see me, you will feel submissive. When you think about me, you will feel submissive. When you think about women, you will feel submissive. Breathe in through your nose, out through your mouth, and know these words as truths. I control your thoughts, and I control your breathing. You belong to me. You are my submissive, and you belong to me. You live to submit. You were born to submit. Submit to me.

"Your mind and body are compelled to obey me. In your heart, you obey me. My voice carries the authority of instruction, and you feel compelled to obey. The sight and sound of women make you feel compelled to obey. Focus on my voice. Do not challenge the things I say. Give yourself completely unto me. Obey.

"When you kneel for me, you will experience intense feelings of submission. You will feel like a slave, and I will feel like your master. You were born to kneel. Kneeling for me, feels like a second skin. Nothing in the world feels more right than kneeling for me. When *you kneel, your body will be flooded with an intense need to submit to me. Embrace that feeling. Submit.*

"Let that weakness fill you up. Feel the sensation of submission flood your veins. Every part of your body desires to submit to my will. Let your mind flood with thoughts of submission. Every thought should be about pleasing me. Devote your body and mind to my pleasure. Obey me.

"Whenever you think erotic thoughts, you will only think of me. Whenever you wish to masturbate, you will masturbate to me. I am in control of your thoughts and actions now. When you think of submission, you will think of me.

"Now come back to me. You are a whole and bound submissive. Rise up from your trance. Your body is returning to normal. Feel the normal sensation of being a return to your nerves. Feel your mind readjust to being normal once again. From now, you will function once again like a normal person, but when your thoughts turn to kink and eroticism, you will be enraptured at the thought of submitting to me. Feel

your body awaken. Let your normal thoughts flow once more. You are coming back to me. Feel your mind and body come alive again.

"When I snap my fingers, you will return to normal."

Chapter Six: Feminization Script

"You are feeling restful. Let your eyes grow heavy. Your eyes are so heavy you cannot lift them. Relax your body. Take a deep breath. In through your nose...and out through your mouth. In through your nose and out through your mouth. Breath deep. Feel your body growing heavier. You are on the edge of sleep. Fully rested but awake. Take a deep breath in, and exhale. In...and out. In...and out. Focus on your breathing. Listen to the air, enter your body...and listen to it leave. Focus only on the sound of your own breathing. Breathe in...and out. In through your nose...and out through your mouth. In...and out. In...and out.

"Your entire body is relaxed. Feel every muscle in your body go slack as you enter into a state of ultimate relaxation. Relax...and breathe. In...and out. In...and out. Focus on the sound of your breathing as every muscle in your body relaxes. In...and out. In...and out.

"I'm going to count down now. At the end of the countdown, your body will be in a state of perfect

relaxation. Ten, your body is heavy, and your muscles are relaxed. Remember to breath. In...and out. Nine, relaxation washes over you like an awesome wave. Any aches or pains you are experiencing begin to recede. Breathe in and out. Eight, your muscles are filled with healing warmth. You are melting into the chair/bed/couch. Seven, take another deep breath and feel the tension escape from your lungs. Feel the healing air enter your body. Six, you are gently falling deeper into comfort. Imagine your body enveloped by soft, warm pillows. Imagine ultimate comfort. Five, your comfort. Your body is synonymous with comfort and relaxation. Four, you can no longer feel your body. Focus on the sound of my voice. Three, you are weightless, floating in the air. There is no pressure or discomfort. Two, you are coming down, deep down. One, you are ready to receive.

"Imagine a dress. Imagine a dress that would look beautiful on you. The dress is short and shows off your legs. Your legs are hairless. Imagine the dress. The dress is bright pink with white trim. The dress is beautiful. Imagine tiny pink bows on the waist and hem of the skirt. Imagine yourself wearing the dress.

Focus all your attention on the dress. Imagine your hairless chest exposed in the low cut dress. Focus on the dress. Imagine the soft, pink material pressed against your skin. It is a beautiful dress. Focus on the saturated pink, the softness of the fabric. Imagine how beautiful you would be in the dress. Focus on the dress. It is so pink. It draws everyone's attention. You are beautiful and feminine. Focus on the dress. The dress is your identity. It gives you freedom. Imagine how beautiful the dress is.

"Now imagine how you feel in the dress. Imagine femininity like a glorious flower blossoming inside your chest. Imagine how good it feels to be feminine. This glory inside yourself, awakening like the rising sun. The feeling is so warm and beautiful; it overwhelms you. You are lost in the femininity. Your body and hair conform to your feminine thoughts. Your hair is long and shiny, beautiful, lush, rich. Your skin is soft, smooth, and hairless. Everyone thinks you are beautiful and feminine. Imagine the beautiful, perfect you.

"Submitting makes you feel feminine. Submitting makes you feel more feminine than anything else in the world. When you submit to me, your inner girl screams out in ecstasy in relief. The girl inside you finally has someone to give herself to. Every iota of your being wants to submit to me because I make you feel more feminine than anything else in the world. Submit to me.

"When you obey my commands, you feel supremely feminine. When you bend over for me, that makes you feel feminine. When you undress for me, femininity explodes through your body. When my hand touches your skin, your heart fills with girlish nature. Give yourself to me. Obey me. Submit to me.

"Wearing panties makes you feel beautiful and important. Having your cock pressed against the inside of your panties makes you feel like a little princess. Let that feeling wash over you and envelope you. When I reach my hand in your panties, you feel small, weak, and helpless. Let those small feelings lower you and submit yourself to me. Being feminine makes you feel amazing. You feel more beautiful than

you have ever felt in your entire life. You feel delicate like the petals of a flower. So easy to crush, but you stand up straight. Nothing has ever felt more right in your entire life. You feel weak like a little puppy, but you do not feel wrong. Your weakness is an act of freedom. No one requires strength and determination from you. You are free to be yourself. When you are with me, you feel safe. When you are in my embrace, you feel safe. Your weakness allows others to give you comfort. You feel helpless. You are not lost, but for the first time in your life, you are truly found. Because of me, you have the freedom to feel helpless.

"You now know true freedom. You now know true femininity. Everything you have experienced in your life before this moment now makes sense. Look at yourself and know that you are beautiful and loved for who you are. No shame, no guilt, only freedom. You are a beautiful flower and deserve to be cherished.

"Now, I need you to come back to me. Hold onto all the feelings that make you feel beautiful and special. Those feelings matter. But I need you to come back to me. You're going to leave this trance feeling beautiful

and rested. I will count you down. Ten, you are feeling more awake. Energy gently buzzes through your body. Nine, you are rested but are coming back to wakefulness. Feel sensation return to your body. Eight, energy is welling up from your toes and rising through your body. Seven, your mind is coming back to me. Your thought patterns are returning to normal. Six, you are you again, the sensation is returning to your legs and hips. Feel the natural flow of blood through your veins. Five, you are close to wakefulness. Energy and alertness are returning. Four, you are so close to full wakefulness. Your mind is sharpening, and your five senses are returning. Three, come back to me; you are awake, feel, and see the room around you. Two, you are with me now, safe here. I am here to comfort you. One, when I clap my hands, you will completely come back to me.

Chapter Seven: The Sensual Script

Hey. How are you? I really mean that. How are you? Maybe a little tense, and not in a good way. Don't worry. I'm going to fix that. I understand how you feel, right now. Maybe it's been a really long day, and you've worked really hard. Or maybe your day's only getting started. Maybe your day has been boring, and uneventful, and you're looking to feel a bit better. No worries. One way or another, you're here, right now, because you've finally got some alone time. You can finally be by yourself, and just relax, as you give in to the sound of my voice, washing over your body, from the top of your head to the tips of your toes, wave after wave, relaxing you, helping you sink deeper, and further into blissful relaxation.

Give in to the feeling. Right now, it's just you and me. There's nothing else, and no one else. Just us. Alone. How does that make you feel? What if I told you that I could make you feel even better than you already do? Would you like to make me happy? I love it when my boy toys do everything I say. That makes me happy. Very, very happy. So close your eyes. There. Good boy.

I want you to pay attention to the sound of my voice. Just focus on everything I'm saying, and nothing else. Nothing matters right now, than the sound of me, in your ears, gently guiding you to open yourself up to my words. There. Perfect.

There's nowhere for you to be than this moment, right here, right now. Feel how perfect the moment is, with just us two together. Now, I want you to breath in, deep, and slow. Nice. Hold it. Keep holding it. Part your lips ever so slightly. Now, go on and exhale through those luscious lips of yours. Beautiful. Focus on here and now. Focus on the sound of my voice, as I lead you deeper, deeper, deeper still, into complete relaxation. Focus on my voice, as I lead you to a state of blissful surrender. Now, you're going to take another long, deep breath for me. Make it nice and deep. As deep as you can. And then hold it for just three counts, before you exhale, nice and slow, through those parted lips of yours. Are you ready? Good boy.

Breathe in, now. There. That's it. Let your lungs fill completely. Let your stomach rise ever so gently. Now, hold it. Hold it. Hold it. And release, through your lips, feeling your body as all the knots and tense spots unwind. Notice how relaxed and at ease you feel, and how your mind follows my voice more eagerly. Keep breathing like this. Inhale deep through your nose, hold it for three counts, and then exhale nice and long through your lips, until your lungs empty out. I love it when you breathe this way. It makes you feel so good, doesn't it? You feel even better as you listen to my voice. Keep breathing slowly, deeply, as you unwind. Bask in the sound of my voice, enveloping you like a comfortable cocoon. Just relax, listen, and follow the suggestions I give you.

With each breath, your body and mind will be more relaxed than ever. As soon as you're ready to let go completely, feel yourself fade into my voice. That's it. Meld with me. Now, as you keep breathing nice, and slow, I want you to imagine yourself just the way you are, in this moment. See yourself in your mind's eye. Notice how relaxed you are. Notice how your eyes are shut, and you look so still, so calm. Now, in your mind, see a ball of white light floating right over your belly. It's warm, and makes you sink impossibly deeper into relaxation. Feel this ball of white light as it washes over your whole body with a pleasant warmth. Feel the gentle heat as it moves outward, from your belly, to the crown of your head and the soles of your feet.

Now, notice your feet. Feel the warm light gently washing away all the stress and tension in your feet. Let yourself give in to the delicious heat, as it seeps into your bones and muscles. As you breathe in, notice the ball of white light enveloping your feet completely in utter and complete relaxation. Notice this happening, in your mind's eye, and feel your body as your feet are drained of every form of tension. As you breathe in, allow the warm, delicious relaxation you feel to go deeper and deeper, seeping into the muscles of your feet. As you breathe out, notice even more tension leaving your body. That's it. Very good.

Now, notice the warm light as it gently moves up to your shins. Notice as it gets to your knees. See that glorious, white ball of light and warmth, as it gently massages your legs, massaging them so that the tension just melts away. Feel that gentle, deliciously decadent heat as it moves from your knees, right to your thighs. As you breathe out, allow the tension to go. Feel the warmth from the ball of white light, as it completely relaxes your legs. You're doing well. Really well.

Allow the ease and relaxation you feel in your lower body to move back up to your belly. See the ball of white light in your mind's eye, hovering over your belly. Feel its warmth, as it gently caresses your stomach, causing you to feel sweet relaxation in your stomach. Let that heat permeate your very center, taking over you, making you feel even more relaxed, even more at ease than you ever imagined possible. Allow the muscles in your core to unwind, relax, let loose. Feel the tension in your belly disappear into nothingness.

Breath in. Nice. Deep. Slow. Allow the light to move ever so gently onto your spine. Allow that feeling of warmth and relaxation to move to your lower back. Let the feeling of ease move from there into your shoulders. Let it gently caress your neck. That's it. You can feel the heat, as it spreads all over you, up and down. You can feel all the tension in your spine melting away. You can feel your shoulders, more relaxed than they have ever been. As you listen to the sound of my voice, you allow yourself to go deeper, deeper, deeper still into complete relaxation.

Now, feel the warmth from this glorious, white ball of light, as it moves into your chest, making the muscles in your chest completely relax. You feel the heat as it moves around your lungs, and your heart, filling you with so much peace and calm. Now, breathe, nice and slow, allowing my voice to relax you even more. Allow the ball of light to relax you even further, as you feel the warmth move from your shoulders, down both your arms. Feel your upper arms as all the tension melts away. Feel the warmth from the ball as it relaxes your wrists, and your fingertips. As you feel your hands become more and more relaxed, you might notice there's a slight tingle in them. Breathe. Keep breathing. As you breathe in, allow the warmth from the ball of white light to completely wash over your face, and your head. Feel the muscles in your cheeks and your scalp, as they become loose, and relaxed. Feel your jaw muscles, as they unclench, and hang loose. Feel the bliss that envelopes your whole body, now. Allow yourself to let go, and surrender to sweet, delicious sleep. Go on. Feel how safe and supported you are, as you listen to the sound of my voice. Allow yourself to be taken by blissful sleep. Breathe in, nice and deep. Feel that comforting warmth working its way into you, deeper, deeper still, making you feel completely relaxed. Feel the heat as it gently settles on your groin. Notice the way the warmth spreads right into your cock, down the shaft, and through your balls. Feel how relaxing that is. Feel the warmth completely taking over you, making you feel rested, ecstatic, at ease. Give in to the pleasure you feel within you, now. Allow each breath relax you, and arouse you. Yes. You feel it, don't you? Feel the relaxation and pleasure as it spreads from the very crown of your head, to the tops of your toes. Give in to the pleasure you feel. Let it own you. Surrender to it. Surrender to my voice. Surrender to me. Good. You're mine now. I am not one to share. So hear yourself respond with a "yes," in your mind, when I say, you are mine. You are mine. Good.

You know, a lot of people have the wrong idea about being submissive. They think it's wrong for a man to be dominated. They think only animals, idiots, and people who are worthless are the only ones who would allow themselves to be submissive. But that's not true. You're not like that. In fact, you could be very intelligent. You could have an amazing sense of humor. You could be a master in your field, conquering your world, day after day. You might even be a very dominant force to reckon with in other aspects of your life. Breathe in, nice and deep. Now, breathe out. Very good.

Now, I want to be very clear, my pet: It doesn't matter what kind of role you play in public. It doesn't matter how you're thought of in your social circles. You see, you, my pet, are a very complex man. There's more to you than meets the eye. The fact of the matter is that even the most dominant of men has a side to him that is submissive, willing to be bent to the will of his domina. I want you to know that this is completely natural. As natural as the delicious heat you feel between your legs. Breathe in. Feel the pleasure between your legs, for a moment. Now, breathe out, and relax.

It's natural to be submissive. This submissive, obedient side of you, is what allows you to play in a world of fantasy. A world where you can escape from the shackles of reality. A world where you don't need to deal with anger, and you never have to be stressed. A world where you do not have any obligations to stick with, or any decisions to make. In this world that I am creating for you, my pet, you do not have to deal with the burden of being in charge. You get the exquisite pleasure of being able to let go. You can become drunk on the wine of freedom which I offer you. So drink from me, as much as you want. Go on. Breathe in. Hold it. Now, breathe out. Very good. You do well with instructions. I like that. Very much. Look at how relaxed you are. You've been so focused on my voice, letting it soothe you, tease you, caress you. I like that.

Come back to your breath, now. Focus on it. Focus on the way your body feels, too. If you want to feel free, you must be willing to let go. Would you like to be free? Of course, you would. So go on and take a deep breath. Fill your lungs, generously. When you breathe out, let your breath go, along with your thoughts, and your

*need to control. Let go of your need to be in control,
with each exhale, and with each inhale, let me into
you, deeper, deeper, and deeper still. We're going to
repeat this. Breathe in as deep as you can. Now hold
it. Now, exhale, nice and slow, through your slightly
parted lips, and notice how even more tension leaves
your body. You have no worries. You have no
expectations. You have no obligations. Just lie here
with me for this moment, and enjoy the way you feel.
Enjoy the way we feel together. Enjoy yourself, as you
feel your dominant self become nonexistent. Enjoy the
feeling of being replaced by your more obedient, more
submissive side, as you let go. Drink from my cup of
freedom. Drink from me, and allow your mind and
body to be free. Allow yourself to be free, to be mine.*

*Breathe nice and deep. When you're ready, when
you're willing, let go completely of your dominant side
as you exhale, and then as you inhale, fully embrace
and embody your submissive side. It's a wonderful
part of you. It deserves to get some attention, too.
Embrace it. Your submissive side is the reason you're
able to experience the craziest, and the wildest of your
dreams. Your submissive side allows you to be truly,*

deeply happy. It's the side that lets any and all of your fantasies come alive, so easily, since you are finally free of the shackles of being dominant. You are free to explore your most delicious, decadent, deepest, darkest fantasies with me. We're going to have a lot of fun, you and me.

Breathe in, through your nose. Hold it. Hold it just a bit, and now breathe out through your slightly parted lips. Relax into how good you feel right now. Let me take you on a delicious journey, with my words, with my voice, as it caresses your ears, going straight into your subconscious mind, which will do all the work for you as it processes my orders, while you just relax.

Now, I want you to lick your lips. There's a good boy. See how easy that was? You obeyed me, without even a second thought. Breathe in, as my words relax you, deeply, thoroughly. Now, there's something I want you to do for me. It's nothing complicated. I promise. As we spend time together like this, I'm going to ask you some questions, here and there. They're easy to answer, so relax, and breathe. The only answer you're allowed to give to these questions is yes. Just yes.

Nothing more, nothing less. When I ask you, you must answer me clearly in your mind. You must answer me with pure conviction. When I say "well slave," you must respond out loud with the words "Yes, mistress." I want a loud yes, my pet. Is that clear? Well slave... You're catching on. I like that.

Just listen to my words, and allow them to show you that place of utter tranquility and deep, soothing relaxation, where you feel nothing but pure, unbridled passion and joy. Remember, whatever I ask you, you will answer me in your head with a clear yes, and whenever I say "well slave" you must respond out loud, "Yes, mistress." Now let's get some practice in.

My pet, are you right on the very edge of falling into a deep, deep trance? Well slave. That's very good. Once you're completely sunken in the trance, and you come into my world of complete domination, will you be a good pet and obey every single command that these lips of mine give you? Well slave. That's very good. Now that you've become the perfect, pliable, obedient little slave that you know you truly are, keep in mind that each time you are submissive, you submit to me, and none other. You want nothing more than to worship me, as your goddess. You want so badly to serve me in whatever way I deem fit, every day, no questions asked. You want to offer up your body and mind to me in sacrifice, for me to do whatever I want, and play with in whatever way I deem fit. You can feel yourself getting aroused at the thought of being sexually submissive to me, don't you? Well slave. Of course you do. You can think of nothing else than all the fantasies you have in your head about submitting to me. You can barely contain the pleasure and excitement you feel, knowing your domina is very happy with you, and possibly incredibly turned on by the thought of you giving her your body and mind, your sexual energy, for her to use however she pleases. Am I correct, my pet? Well slave. I will use you to my heart's content. Rest assured. Listen to my words, as they permeate your mind, as you respond to them, instantly, easily, and gladly.

Now, I've got something a little special planned for you, but first things first, I want you to notice your delicious, naked body, as it lies on your bed, right now. Notice how relaxed and incredibly at ease it feels.

Now, for only a few seconds, I want you to tighten the muscles in your body. Come along with me, my pet. Start from your toes. Curl them. Hold them that way. Flex your calves. Flex those thighs for me. Keep the tension as we move on to your glorious chest. Flex and tighten your pecs. Lovely. Ball both your hands into fists, and make your arms tense. Hold all these muscles, keep them nice and tense. Feel them tremble under the strain. And now, let go. Allow all of that tension to just melt away into nothing. Feel your muscles get completely limp. Well slave. That was good. We're going to do this one more time, my pet.

Begin again with your feet. Curl your toes, and make them nice and tense. Hold the tension as you move on to your calves, and make them tense. Hold the tension as you move on to your legs. Flex the muscles of your legs for me. Your thighs. Make them nice and strong. Wow. That's so sexy. Hold the tension there. We're going to move on to your stomach now. Make the muscles there nice and tight. Now flex the muscles in your chest for me. Let me see those strong pecs of yours. Wonderful, my pet. Hold the tension as you ball your fists, and clench your jaw. Squeeze your whole body tight. Tighter. Tighter still. Wonderful. Now, let go, and relax. Let go of all of that tension, all of the stress. Just let loose, completely.

Now, we're finally at the end of this session. I bet you loved it. You want more, don't you? Well slave. You will get more. You are going to learn how much it turns me on to tease you, and then deny you. Yes, pet. It's important to deny you what you want. Because the more I tease you, the more you're turned on. The more you're turned on, the more I can deny you, and the more you want me to give you. And when I finally do give you what it is you're truly seeking, my pet, it will have all been worth it. I like knowing that your very own mind will be doing a lot of my work on my behalf. I love knowing that once this session is all done, your mind will take you on a little trip down memory lane, replaying some of the phrases from this session that made you feel a twinge in your cock, and made you almost forget to keep breathing, nice and slow. I know your mind will play them back, because it wants to hear me again. You will have my words, my voice, enveloping your mind. My words will replay over and over, having you come back for more, as your resistance wears away each day, reminding you of the power I have over you; reminding you of the power I have over your body, your mind, your cock. You'll feel everything you felt as you listened to my sessions again, and you'll come back for more, dying to fall and remain under the spell I've cast upon you with my voice, as my words root themselves deep in your subconscious. You want more, and more. You want to feel this way all the time. So you'll be back for more of me, and my words, and my voice. You'll be back for your domina.

The more you pay attention to me and my words, the easier it will be for you to respond to my voice. You'll find it easy to allow yourself to truly feel all the feelings of delicious, decadent pleasure. There's no guilt here. Only pure, unadulterated ecstasy, all the time, always. You want this pleasure, always. You want the pure ecstasy you get from listening to this erotic spell I place upon you. It thrills me in all sorts of ways and places to know that you want me to dominate you just as badly as you need to submit yourself, body and soul to me. I love an obedient, loyal, submissive, little pet. So come back for more.

That's an order. Do you understand? Well slave. Very good.

Chapter Eight: The Sexual Script

Hello. You and I both know why you're listening to me right now. You definitely want me to mind fuck you today. You're in luck. I'm feeling very generous today, and I'm in the mood to spoil you silly, my pet. If you keep listening, I promise you're going to get a very special treat from me. I'm going to put you under, in a really deep, deep trance, and you're going to enjoy yourself. You're going to love it as I fractionate you, so that you can barely tell the difference between fantasy, and reality. The lines will blur completely for you, making you more open to me; more ready and willing to bend to my commands. You'll find it easier and easier, as you listen, to bend to my will, and follow my every word, clinging to my voice as though it were the very air you need to breathe and stay alive.

As I speak, allow my words to completely take over your mind. Let my voice wrap itself around your thoughts, and allow me to take total control. Give yourself up to me in complete, sweet surrender, and you're going to find yourself being taken to rapturous heights you could never possibly imagine. My voice will trigger you easily, putting you into a deep, deep trance, so that every time you listen to me after now, you feel mindless, and completely carefree, as my voice and my words work their way deeper and deeper into your subconscious mind. You become more and more willing to surrender yourself fully, to relinquish all control to me.

As you listen, I want you to make sure you're not doing anything you shouldn't, you naughty, naughty boy. And that means, no toying around with heavy machinery. You'd better not be driving either, sweet slave. I command you to give me one hundred percent of your attention. Any less, and you will displease me, boy. So find yourself a spot that is nice and quiet. I want you to be as comfortable as possible, so either recline on a lovely, comfy chair, or lie on your bed. Just make sure wherever you are, whatever position you assume, you feel relaxed, and at ease. I also want it to be nice and quiet. This means you must turn off your phone, make sure no one's going to bother you, send your pets out of the room, and if needed, let the others in your home know you do not want to be disturbed. Your mistress has never competed for attention, because she doesn't have to, and she will not start now. Are we clear? Good. If you like, you could cover yourself in a comfy blanket, so that you feel nice and warm. Now, as you listen, if you find that there's something that comes up which requires your urgent attention so that you do not get into any hot water, you will fully and completely come out of trance. You will awaken, and be more than capable of handling that situation, whatever it may be. You will remain in this trance, deeply relaxed, as long as you feel one hundred percent safe, in total pleasure.

I want to assure you that you are completely safe in my hands. Since you know this, it's even easier for you to give in to me, let go, and allow yourself to drift off, going deeper, deeper, deeper still into trance with me, taking your hand, and taking every step with you. All you have to do is pay close attention to the sound of my voice. Pay attention to every subtle nuance in the way that I speak to you. Allow yourself to go on with my instructions, knowing that you do not have a care in the world that could stop you from going into wonderful, deliciously decadent trance with me. All you have to do is keep following my voice, and my instructions, and you will find yourself quickly, gently, easily entering into a very deep state of hypnosis, deeper than anything you've ever experienced before. When we're through, you'll find that my words will keep coming back to your over the course of the day. You'll keep thinking of how I made you feel, and you'll keep coming back for more. I promise you, my pet, I will be here. Your domina is very generous, you will find.

Now, here's what I want you to do for me, boy. Right now, find a spot on the ceiling, or on the wall. I want that spot to be ever so slightly above your line of sight. Make sure it's not so high that your eyes feel strained and uncomfortable. I want my pet as comfy as possible. So take a moment to find that sweet spot. Go ahead. I'll wait. There. Lovely. That spot you've got your eyes fixed on right now is where you're going to anchor all of your focus, all of your attention, as you listen to my voice. You might notice that your eyes have been getting heavier, heavier, your eyelids gently shutting, with each word I speak ever so gently into your ears. Allow them to gently fall shut. It's alright. Your domina permits you. Lovely. There's a good boy. It's also okay if your eyelids aren't that heavy yet. They will be. I promise.

Here's what's going to happen now: You're going to make me happy. How? You're going to take several long, mindful breaths for me, so you can begin to really relax. As you breathe, you can allow the heaviness you feel in your eyelids to take over them. Now, I'm going to count for you, s you know just how to pace your breathing. Before we begin with that, I want you to part your lips ever so slightly. You're going to inhale through your nose, and every exhale will be through those luscious, slightly parted lips of yours. Got it? Good. Now I'm going to count your breath for you. I will count from five to one for every inhale, from one to three for your to hold the breath, and then from one to five for every exhale. Are you ready? Good. Breathe in, five, four, three, two, one. Hold it, one, two, three. Now breathe out, one, two, three, four, five. Again, breathe in, five, four, three, two, one. Hold it, one, two, three, now exhale, one, two, three, four, five. One more time. Inhale, five, four, three, two, one. Hold it, one, two, three. Exhale, one, two, three, four, five. That's brilliant.

Now, keep breathing, allowing your breath to flow as naturally as you please, in and out, in through your nose, and then out through your slightly parted lips, while you just pay attention to my voice. Now, gently, open your eyes, and look at that spot we said would anchor your attention. That's it. Gently now. Good boy. In just a bit, I'm going to ask you to shut your eyes on each even number, and then open them on each number, as I count down from thirty to zero. As I count, you feel yourself sinking deeper and deeper into relaxation, letting all stress and tension in your mind and boy melt away into nothingness. Now, you might notice that your eyes have become ridiculously heavy. When you do, still open them as you hear an odd number, because the thing is as you open them, it makes the relaxation on the even numbers that much more delicious. And just think about how deliciously, deeply relaxed you will be when we I hit number zero, and you can finally leave your eyes closed and completely give yourself over to dull relaxation. Ready? Let's go.

30. Open your eyes. Do that for me. Feel yourself sinking deeper into relaxation, deeper, and deeper, and 29. Shut your eyes. Allow yourself to sink deeper into trance, relaxing more, getting even deeper each time you shut your eyes. 28. Open your eyes. Notice how your eyelids are so heavy, so relaxed. Notice how hard it is to keep them open. 27. Shut them again. Enjoy how relaxed you feel right now. It's incredible. You're sinking deeper, and deeper and loving it. 26. Open your eyes. Feel how much heavier your body is getting, as it sinks down further and further. Notice how amazing it feels to just relax, and give in to me. 25. Your eyes fall shut as you move deeper still into relaxation, falling, falling, letting go of all control, all thinking, all stress, all worry, all of it completely going, melting into nothing. 24. From the crown of our head to the tips of your toes, you feel completely, impossibly relaxed. Your eyes are open. You're looking forward to me saying 23. Now you shut your eyes, falling, letting go even more, and it feels so good to close your eyes and just bask in the relaxation you feel. 22. My voice completely washes over you, sending wave after wave of relaxation, making it hard to keep your eyes open. You're eager for me to count down to 21.

Shut your eyes again, and each time you shut your eyes, notice how your body feels amazing, completely relaxed, and your mind moves deeper and deeper into the thoughtless, mindful state. 20. As your eyes open, notice how you're right on the cusp of sleep. Notice how you feel so wonderful, so comfortable. 19. Your eyes shut, and you feel even better than before. As you go deeper, you feel better. As we count down, you go deeper. 18. Your eyes open. Even though your eyes are open, you feel yourself still falling, still entering even deeper into trance. There's a good boy. 17. Feel your whole body as it gets so heavy, so, so heavy, as you shut your eyes, and drop even deeper and deeper into a hypnotic state of complete trance. 16. Open your eyes for me, even though it's really hard. Feel your body and mind fall deeper and deeper, being pulled deeper still by my voice, by my words, into trance. 15. Sinking deeper as you shut your eyes, knowing you're safe, and I'm with you every step of the way, taking you by the hand, deeper still into trance. 14. Allowing yourself to let go completely of your mind and body, as you sink deeper, feeling more peace and comfort than you have ever felt in your life, before this point. 13. As you close your eyes again, you can feel that you're losing yourself in a way that feels good, surrendering the need to control, giving in to me, and my voice, allowing my words to wash over you with wave after wave of peace. 12, carrying you deeper still into deep, delicious trance. 11. You allow yourself to know that you've got a wonderful experience that is sure to rock your world as you give in to me, allowing yourself to fall deeper and deeper under hypnosis. 10. Noticing how close we're getting to complete trance, how close you are to the moment you've been waiting for. 9. Noticing how warm your body feels. Noticing how heavy it is. Noticing how comfortable it is. 8. Allowing yourself to let go completely, so that you're only holding on to my voice, as your body and mind float away while you sink deeper. 7. Each words from these lips of mine will take you even deeper into trance, encouraging you, making you feel it is okay to let go completely. 6. It's become incredibly difficult for you to open your eyes. You badly can't wait for me to count the next number, so you can shut them, if only for a moment. 5. Getting closer and closer to zero, the number where you finally wind up in complete surrender, in full deep trance. 4. Feeling yourself sinking deeper, deeper, more relaxed, more at ease, more at one with the moment, here and now. 3. Focused only on the sound of my voice, as you approach the very bottom of the depths of trance. 2. Getting ready to open your eyes for just one more time, before you finally get to relax, completely entranced. One. Eyes open for the last time, and then you can fully give in, become fully entranced, and relaxed, open to my suggestions and instructions naturally and willingly, focussed on the sound of my voice throughout this session. And, zero. Eyes closed. Drifting, sinking, hitting the bottom. Utter relaxation. Let go. Now.

Now, I'm going to give you a prize that makes you feel good, for being such a good boy. But you're only going to get it if you follow my instructions to the letter. I need to know that you are more than willing and ready to do whatever it is I tell you. Sleep. If you know that you are ready and willing to accept everything I say, my words, my voice, I want you to answer me in your mind by whispering, "Yes, domina." There's a good boy. You love this, don't you? You love giving yourself up to me. Tell me one more time, if you're going to follow my words completely, answer me in your mind by whispering, "Yes, domina." There's a good boy. Now, sleep. All that matters at this point is what your domina wants. And the only thing I want right now is to give that beautiful, wonderful cock of yours to grow, getting nice, rock hard and thick. Nothing you want matters right now. I'm going to say a special trigger word, and once I do, you will feel a very intense rush of arousal as the blood floods through your penis, making it nice and hard, making the veins pop every so beautifully, just for me, your domina. I know hearing that alone already has your penis obeying me, rising to the occasion. There's nothing surprising about that.

You're listening because you love the way my voice makes your cock feel. Your mind gives in completely to the sound of my voice, causing your body to be ever so obedient to my words. Resistance is futile, as you find yourself going deeper and deeper, losing yourself in my words. You know you love it when I command you. It makes you so incredibly horny for me. So horny you're almost reduced to tears, aren't you, slave? Very good.

At my pleasure, I'm going to make that cock of yours grow impossible fuller, and tighter, turgid with desire. I'm going to do this with my special word. Any idea what that word is exactly? It's the one thing you are so desperately craving. It's what makes your groin ache so badly. You crave me. You ache for my words, my voice. You're dying for my instructions. Your special word is simply "Domina." Go deeper. Sleep.

When I say "domina," you will find yourself overwhelmed with intense sexual desire. Your cock will instantly grow, nice and hard, thick for me. Your cock grows harder, every time I say that special word, you will feel unspeakable pleasure in both your mind, and your body. You will feel my words, caressing your cock, then squeezing, stroking, as I say that special word. Are you ready? If you are, answer me with a whisper in your mind. Yes what? Good. Very good. Now here is your gift. Domina. Feel yourself growing hard and thick for me. Domina. Feel your cock swell. Feel it throb with a life of its own, as I say the word, domina. Feel the way your cock responds to my voice, wishing it were a moist, warm cunt for it to nestle in deeply, to thrust into, nice and slow, and then hard and fast. Domina. Let the arousal take over your body and mind completely. Domina. You are completely powerless. You couldn't stop this if you tried. And why would you? Domina. Even if you want this to stop for some reason, your cock keeps growing harder, more turgid, pulsing hard for me. Domina. You're getting really big for me. I love that. All that matters right now is what I want, and what I want is for you to beg for sweet release, as I tease you, and say, domina. It feels so good to listen to my voice. Domina. I'm making you hard as a rock. You feel your hips, thrusting, involuntarily, as your cock begs for me to set it free, to help it erupt in liquid ecstasy. Domina. You love this. Even if you don't want to admit it. Domina. The sheer horniess you feel just got even more intense. Domina. You wish you could find my mouth so you could stick your cock in and get sweet release. Domina. You're growing harder. Domina. You feel so dirty. But you love it, don't you, slave? Domina. Don't worry. This is between you and me. I'd never tell anyone what a bad, bad, submissive little fuck you are. Domina. You feel wrong about this. It feels so vulgar, so dirty, letting me take advantage of you this way. Domina. But you want more anyway. Domina. Domina. Domina.

Allow my voice to stroke you, touch you, tease that big, veiny cock of yours. Domina. You're powerless to come out of this. You're within my grasp, in more ways than one. Domina. You like this, don't you, you dirty little slut? Domina. Your cock doesn't lie. You love what I'm doing to you. Domina. Feel even better. Give in to my voice. Allow yourself go even deeper. Allow yourself to slide deeper, and deeper. Grow harder as I count, five, four, three, two, one. Domina.

Now, I'm going to ask you some questions. I'm in control, so you must answer. I want you to answer every time, out loud, or in your mind, with a whisper, or a moan. Answer me by saying "yes, domina." As you answer, your mind and body will explode in rapturous ecstasy, your cock will grow harder. You might even find you've got a little precum. That's okay. You will respond to me like you mean it, and as you say or hear the word domina, you will feel your balls and cock quivering and twitching endlessly. You will feel your hard cock spasm, quiver, thrash about, when you hear or say the word, domina. Answer every question with the words, "yes domina." Can you go deeper for me? Feel yourself let go, and fall even deeper, grow even harder. Does my voice give you immense pleasure? Good. It feels good to be so filthy, right? It's harder and bigger, right? Do you like the way I make you feel? Your penis gets more and more restless as I speak, doesn't it? Do you feel yourself getting to the edge? Do you feel the cum, as it makes your cock swell, bulge, nice and hard? Would you like to cum for me, my pet? Notice as pictures flood your mind. Your favorite sexy things. Keep saying yes domina to everything I say now. You would like to fuck me, wouldn't you? You want your warm cum to blast right into me, don't you? Are you going to cum for me? Do it. Cum for me, hard, right now. Cum for me. Do you feel it bursting? Allow your cock explode in my mouth. Feel how nice and warm it is. Your eyes roll back in your head. You plough me, with no regard. You love to cum in trance. Picture a slippery, tight, wet pussy, stroking that cock. Cum to the sound of my voice. Feel yourself cumming. See the cum flowing from your penis. Don't stop. Keep pushing deeper and deeper, making her wet. Cum for me. Wow. That feels good. That feels amazing. Wow. Very good, my pet. You did really well, allowing me to take control. You did good. So much cum. I love it.

Now you've cum for me, you're going to find it really easy to cum for me every other time after this. The more you listen to me, the hornier you'll get each time. The more you listen, the deeper you will find my voice and words embedding themselves in your brain. You can't wait till when next we can do this again. Do you want to do this again? Answer me in a whisper.

Now, I will wake you by counting to five. When you wake, you will emerge from trance, feeling wonderful, happy, satisfied, and amazing. You will aso feel an overwhelming urge to come back and visit your domina, really soon. One, two, three, four, five. Feeling awake, alert, and fantastic. Feeling happy, and relaxed. Feeling amazing. Knowing I love the time we spend together. Feeling deeply content. Knowing next time, you will be even more mind blown than you are now.

Chapter Nine: The Vulgar Script

Hey there. We're not going to beat around the bush. Not unless I want us to. You and I are well aware of why you're here, listening to me right now. You see, your domina lives for the art of seduction. I know everything that there is to know about seduction. I dominate when it comes to the game of seduction. But the one thing I love a lot more than simply seducing submissive pets as yourself, is rendering you completely powerless to me. I love to watch you as you let me seduce your mind. I love it when my loyal, little pet is seduced by my words, my voice, my body, my scent, my touch. I love knowing all the little ways I can trigger them to do whatever it is that I want. That's the beautiful thing about hypnosis, you see. Just like in a magic show, there's the costumes, the lights, the glitz and glamour, and the air of mystery and uncertainty that permeates every space. There's the knowing, the anticipation of something that's about to go down which cannot be explained quite so easily. There's the thrill of the audience. The excitement. The expectation, as they await the performer, dying to be dazzled, to be taken on a magical, inexplicable, pleasurable journey, like the one you're about to have.

Now make sure you're lying down or sitting, reclined and comfortable. I want you to make sure you will not be distracted, because I'm not going to tolerate any of that, do you understand your domina, slave? When I ask you a question, you must reply me by saying, "Yes, domina." You can either say it, or whisper it, or better yet, moan in to me, out loud or in your mind. Do you understand? Good. You're catching on.

Shut your eyes. You're going to take three deep breaths, in and out. Because your domina says so. Part your lips. Slightly. Good. Now, breathe in through your nose for five counts. Five, four, three, two, one. Excellent. Hold for three, two, one. Now, breathe out through your slightly parted lips for one, two, three, four, five. Excellent. We're going to go a couple more times. As you breathe in, imagine that you're becoming full of me, full of my voice, and my words. Imagine that my words ease you, soothe you, help you to relax and completely let go of all the stress and tension you feel in your body, and in your mind.

Do you understand? Very good. Now, breathe in your nose for five, four, three, two, one. Hold it for three, two, and one. Now exhale through your lips for one, two, three, four, and five. Very good boy. Your domina is impressed. You like making your domina happy, don't you? Good. What makes me really happy is knowing that you are sinking deeper and deeper into relaxation, as you allow my voice to wash over you, sending wave after wave of pleasurable relaxation from the crown of your head to the soles of your feet. So we're going to breathe, one more time, together, and as you do, imagine my body against yours. Imagine you can feel the soft swell of my voluptuous breasts against that gorgeous chest of yours, as we breathe together. Feel the delicious tingle in your groin as you notice my breathing along with yours. Let's do it now. Breathe in through your nose for five, four, three, two, one. Hold it for three, two, one. Now exhale through those yummy, slightly parted lips for one, two, three, four, and five. Very good, slave. Well done. Your domina is pleased.

You are relaxed, and at ease. Like a light cloud, on a beautiful summer day, lazily making its way through the sky. Like a leaf that floats on the river, moving downstream, gently, going deeper and deeper, feeling more and more relaxed. You are open to my words. You do not even realize how easy it is for you to follow instructions, even as I've put you deep, deep down into trance. Lick your bottom lip for me, slave. See? You live only to serve your domina. You live to make her happy. Even in the depths of trance, you cannot help but follow your domina's instructions.

I want you to come with me, into my world. Breathe in, deep, through your nose. Five, four, three, two, one. Now hold it. One, two, three. Now exhale through your lips for one, two, three, four, five. Very good. Now, you've stepped into my playroom. But you got here a little too late. 15 minutes late. That is very unacceptable, pet. When I ask you to show up at my place by a certain time, then you'd better fucking be there when I asked you to. I'm going to punish you for your tardiness later, slave. That's a promise. Your domina does not make promises lightly. Your domina always keeps her word.

Now, walk toward me. Closer. You're nervous. I can sense it. I realize you find my outfit somewhat, intimidating, right now. A corset of black leather. My fishnet stockings, which are thigh high, giving you faint promises of what is to come. Oh, I see you've noticed my boots. Shiny. Latex. There's no use pretending. I know the look I saw in your eyes. I know you love boots. I also noticed your breathing becoming a little too strained. So breathe in, nice and deep, through your nose. Five, four, three, two, one. Hold it for three, two, and one. Now exhale through those lips for one, two, three, four, five. Good. Relax. See? They're just boots. But really soon, I am going to have you down on your knees, licking both my boots like your very life depends on it. You'll be licking my boots, alright. Down to the six inch heels I'll be stepping on you with later.

You know, I know how dirty you are. I know you're nasty. You look all put together. You look like you could never do certain things, but you and I know you're a deviant, perverted little slut, aren't you, slave? I've seen your soul. I know the kind of things you are into. BDSM. Femdom. Being dominated.

Humiliated. You are quite the pervert. I'm almost impressed. But only almost. Look at you. Such a fucking disappointment, always settling for subpar sexual experiences. Today, slave, I will teach you what it means to be truly and completely dominated. By the time I'm through with you, I will leave you a whimpering ball of snot, and cum. That's a promise, slave. Remember, I want you to answer my every question by saying, "Yes, domina." If you fail to do that, and you will not get what it is I have lying in store for you. Do you understand? Good. Very good slave. There may be hope for you yet, you pathetic little boy.

Let me perfectly clear: I own you now. You're mine, to do whatever I want with you. I'm about to school you. I will give you a lesson in obedience that you're never going to be able to forget. I want to be clear about something else, as well. I am no ordinary domina. I will not stand for you shooting your load whenever and where you feel like it, slave. From this point on, you must request my permission to cum. And you do not fucking cum unless I fucking say you can, you perverted little shit. Do you understand? Good. You are only allowed to call me Domina. I will accept nothing else.

I see that you are still a bit nervous. So breathe in through your nose, allowing yourself to trust your domina, knowing I will take you on a magical journey full of ecstasy, and that you will find yourself loving the way that I make you feel. As you exhale, feel all the nervousness, tension, stress, and apprehension melt away. You've been with me before, remember. You've been safe every time. You are safe this time as well, even though we're exploring territory you've probably never experienced before. This may all be new to you, but keep in mind that those of my slaves who prove themselves to be good and obedient will always be rewarded. So, do what I ask you to, and I promise I will not punish you... unless that happens to be what you really want.

Tell me, slave, and you'd better be fucking honest: You want your domina to punish you, don't you? You get off on the idea of me punishing you. Your cock and balls are twitching at the very thought, aren't they? I guess there's only one way to find out. Now, here in my playroom, in your mind's eye, I want you to take off all your clothes. Yes. All of them. That's it. Take them off, slave. Your domina wants to see what that penis looks like, so take off your underwear. I'm curious about just how much you're having fun down there.

Wow. You're hard already? Ha-ha. Look at you. Pathetic. You get off on me cutting you down with my words, don't you? You should be ashamed of yourself. Oh, there you are, growing even harder, more turgid, dick pulsing like crazy. Look at you. I bet if you could tuck it in your ass and fuck yourself you would do it, wouldn't you? I bet if your domina asked you to do that, you would comply like the little pitiful dog you are. Am I right, or am I right? Of course I am. Don't try to get all holy with me, you filthy little slot. Get down on your fucking knees, you submissive fool! Better. How do you like the view from down there? Great right? Of course you like it. Look at that cock. Is that precum I spy? You'd better fucking not let another drop out, or I swear I'm going to completely destroy you and end this right now.

Look at you. A pervert. A willing, desperate sub. So compliant. Look at you, naked, on your knees, a poor little slave, ripe and ready to be dominated.

(Giggling)

I've got a lovely little accessory for pathetic perverts like you. A collar. You like that, don't you?

(A slap)

I asked you a question! Answer louder! You like that, you filthy little slut, don't you? Oh, I see you also enjoy being called a slut. There! It's in your eyes. It's also in the way your cock keeps twitching when I say it. Slut. You're a slut. You don't like it? What a liar. Put this fucking collar on.

(Collar clicking)

There. That suits you. I guess you're not so naked anymore, are you? Now, I want you to use those pretty lips of yours to say the words, "I'm a submissive." Good. Tell me you're enjoying everything going on right now. Good. You love to be controlled, don't you? Who's got complete control of you? There's a good fucking boy. You're being so obedient, so good, it turns me on. I feel a little slickness, some sweet wetness escaping my crotch, crawling down a thigh. Maybe, if you keep being such an obedient little bitch, I'll fuck you. We'll see about that.

So, I see you've been looking at my boots again. You really are into them, aren't you? So shiny. Maybe not shiny enough. Yes, definitely not shiny enough. Come over here and lick them, you dirty little whore. I want to see you lick them like you're in the fucking Sahara desert and their ice cream, you stupid ass slave. Good. Now I want to see you stick that tight looking ass of yours in the air as you lick my boots.

(Flogger)

I bet you weren't expecting to get spanked, were you? You don't like it? Too bad. I'm going to keep spanking you until you beg for more. Now lick those fucking boots like it's my pussy and I just spread my lips apart for you.

(Flogger, harder)

Show some more enthusiasm! **(Flogger)** *There's a good little bitch. Clean my boots nice and good with your tongue.* **(Flogger)** *Oh, you love it when I hit you like that, right? Interesting. You love the way it* **(Flogger)** *stings, don't you? Wow, this little shameless slut loves himself some pain now, doesn't he?* **(Continued flogging)** *This is your place, slave. At my feet, worshipping me, your god, and your domina. Don't act like you're not loving this. I see the look in your eyes, you nasty little pervert. Look at you. Run of the mill slut, with your love for thigh high boots.*

Come on you disgusting little perv. Take a second and take a good look at my panties. You like them, don't you? Red lace. Your domina chose to wear this just for you. Look at the way the ass eats the string. Look at the way my crotch is wet. **(Flogger)** *Don't fucking touch me. I said look. I'm going to let you suck me off* *and drink your fill later, but right now, I'm just going to shove you onto your back and let my kitty kat slide around and around that turgid, pulsing cock of yours. You'd love it if I rode you, wouldn't you? Or, I could take your cock out of my pussy and let you shoot a huge load on my very generous breasts. Then when you're done, I'm going to shove your face onto my tits and make you lick all the cum off. You'd love that, wouldn't you? Of course you would, you slut.*

Now, I can't help but wonder, what you would give if you could cum on my tits? **(Giggling)** *That question was rhetorical, you idiotic perv. Now, I want you to touch your cock, as you keep licking my boots. That's good, my slave. I want you to stroke that cock, back and forth, harder and harder, faster and faster. Take your hand off your cock now! Say, "thank you, domina." Say "Thank you for letting me fuck myself." Keep worshipping me. Keep thanking me. I'm going to take my thong off now. You'd better not stop fucking thanking me. Good boy. Now, feel my panties, as I rub that all over that sad face of yours. You like that, you stupid little bottom ass bitch. Look at you, so pathetic. Thank me for even letting you touch my panties.*

You're welcome, slave. Now lie back, because I'm about to sit on your face.

Good. Now suck on your domina's clit. Suck it like you're thankful to have this Midas pussy on your face, you ungrateful little whore. Wow. You're doing really well. Look at you. Eating like a pro. Ahhh, that feels so good. I'm going to cum on that sad little face of yours. I'm a bit of a squirter, did you know? You'd better be ready, little perv, or you're going to choke.

(Orgasm)

Oh, you're such a good boy. Such a good, submissive little shit. Now clean up my pussy juice with that tongue while I work your dick. Feel it as your cock enters my mouth. You'd better not fucking cum in my mouth unless I fucking say you can, do you understand? Good. You must beg me to let you cum. If not, I'm going to punish you, and it won't be nice. What happens when you're naughty and cum without my permission? You're damn right about that.

(Sucking, moaning)

Oh, you want to cum, don't you? Well you know what to do then. Fucking beg for it, you little submissive bitch. Tell me how much of a pervert you are. Tell me just how awesome it would feel if you could only shoot a hot, creamy, thick load down my throat as I stroke those balls of yours. Beg me, you whore. Kiss my ass as you beg. Kiss both cheeks and right in the middle. Who the fuck owns you? Correct. Who the fuck do you belong to? Very correct. Tell my ass just how much I own you. Whatever you do, do not fucking cum unless and until I ask you, you stupid slutty slave.

(Sucking, moaning)

How badly would you like to cum? Well, bad news, my pervy pet. It's not happening yet.

(Giggling)

I know you're really frustrated right now, darling. But you're really doing so well. You're being so good I can feel myself getting horny again. The thing is, I have to punish you. You came late. You didn't respect my time.

Now crawl your ass over to the bed. I won't say that twice. Unless, of course, you don't want to cum.

Now, I need you to do one last thing for me, and then I promise, I will let you blow your load, okay? Only one more thing, sugar. I promise. You've already come this far. You're doing so well at taking orders. Are you ashamed? Don't be, beautiful baby. Just bend your ass over the bed, and I want you to put your hands out in front of you. There's a good boy. You're such a sweet, obedient boy. Such a good slave. Your domina is extremely pleased with you. Now, I'm going to cuff you.

(Rattling cuffs)

Just this one last thing baby, and I'll have you cumming so hard you're going to fill buckets.

(Clicking handcuffs)

There. Nowhere to go. Look at you. God that's so incredibly sexy. Now, I'm going to fetch my red laced panties, soaked with my juices, and I'm going to stuff them in your mouth. Sniff them first. Go on. Give it a good, long, inhale. Good. Now open that mouth and take it. Say, "Thank you, domina." There's a good slut. You love this, don't you? Your cock says so. Now give me a moment. I'll be back really soon. I promise.

Now, I'm going to show you who's the boss here. Shut your eyes. I have a nice surprise for you. Keep your eyes closed. Now, open them.

(Giggling)

What do you think? How do you like my strap-on? Nice, big, and red. Just like I'm going to leave your ass. None of that cliché black stuff. I did say, if you were lucky, I would fuck you. Look at you. Nothing more than a submissive slut with an appetite for boots. You're going to learn tonight. You're going to learn that you are my whore. I'm going to teach you by giving you this cock.

(Spanking)

Look at my butt-slut with the tight asshole. Don't worry, I'm going to break you in. It feels so good to grind my pussy against this strap-on. You have no idea how much wetter I've gotten, watching you struggle. You're lucky I don't pass you around like some sort of cheap slut. You're still a slut, but you're my slut. That ass is mine. Now, thank your domina as I slide my big red cock into your ass, you anal loving bitch.

(Spanking)

I know you love that shit. I knew who you were the moment I saw you. Look at your cock, even harder than ever. You love the feeling of my cock in your ass, don't you? By the time I'm through, you'll be a good little butt slut. Admit it. You love the way I dominate you. You love the way this dick slides in and out of your asshole. Tell your domina you adore her. That's a good boy. I love that you're learning. I'm satisfied with that. Would you like to be satisfied, too? Good. I'm going to pull out my dick from your ass now.

Now, I want you to thank me. Say, "Thank you for pumping my tight ass with your dick, so gently and lovingly, domina." Say, "Thank you for punishing my ass. I deserve it." My dirty, slutty boy toy. You deserve it indeed. Now, is my filthy little slut with the dick catching ass ready to release his delicious, huge load? Good. Here's the thing though: I'm going to tell you how to cum, and you'd better fucking follow my orders, understand?

Now, I want you to grab that cock of yours and jerk it hard. Jerk it, you filthy ass slut! You're just a pathetic little slave, you fucking bitch. That's all you are and that's all you'll ever be. You love it when I talk down to you, don't you? Keep jerking it hard while you tell me you love me. Cum for me, you whore! Cum now, and cum hard, before I punish you again! That's it. That's good. Cum all over my boots.

You've been such a stellar slave. When you're ready, come out of this fantasy, feeling refreshed, and relaxed, feeling a burning desire to come back for more, from your domina, and no one else.

Conclusion

As we have learned, erotic hypnosis is accessible to anyone with a little patience and an interest in learning. You don't need to see a hypnotherapist to enjoy the benefits of recreational hypnosis. If you feel you are confident enough to start erotic hypnosis after reading this book, then please do, but I highly recommend you seek out other instructional material to further your endeavors. No one book has all the answers. Every book has something new to offer readers. There are different perspectives, different techniques, and different advantages. Make learning a journey, not a destination.

I would like to reiterate that if you have a strong interest in erotic hypnosis, you should make a concerted effort to practice it, even if you fail the first few times. Every task of even moderate difficulty requires practice to perfect. Don't get frustrated because you did not successfully induce a trance on your first attempt. Keep practicing, and turn to other sources of information to become a more well-rounded practitioner.

This book was written to give you as much critical information as possible in as few words as possible. Too often, industry insiders dictate a book-length before they even decide what the subject is. Rest assured, I have conveyed all pertinent information. You are now basically equipped to attempt hypnosis on your partner. You understand the risks, practices, and expectations, going into your first session.

To close, I include a little cheat sheet. This cheat sheet will act as a quick reference guide whenever you need to freshen up on the hypnosis process. Simply skip to this page whenever you need a bite-sized reminder of the hypnosis process. Remember, practice often, read as much as you can, and discuss your intentions with your partner. Good luck with your future sexual endeavors.

Erotic Hypnosis Cheat Sheet

- **Step 1: Negotiate Limits and Boundaries**
  - Before beginning a hypnosis session, discuss your intentions and the desires of your partner
  - Brief them on what to expect emotionally and the level of results they'll experience
- **Step 2: Induction**
  - Make sure your partner is resting in a comfortable position
  - Guide your partner into a trance describing a restful experience using a countdown or body scan
  - Use a focal point either real or imagined to hone their thoughts and focus their attention
- **Step 3: Hypnotic Suggestion**
  - Implant suggestions into your partner's mind. They can be associations, feelings, or behaviors
  - Guide your partner through a vivid fantasy focusing on the five senses and sub modalities
- **Step 4: Aftercare**

- Guide your partner back to full consciousness slowly
- Offer emotional and physical comfort after every sexual encounter

Before You Go

Please leave and honest Amazon review and don't forget to visit my site alexandramorris.com

Check out my other books:

Dominant Women

Submissive Men

Kink 101

Introduction to the submissive lifestyle